Grouping Living Things

by Patricia Walsh

What is a classification system?

Let's say you've just returned from grocery shopping. You bring the shopping bags into the kitchen. Now, where do all these things go? Let's put the frozen food away first. Frozen vegetables go into the freezer. Eggs, milk, and cheese go into the refrigerator. Canned foods go on the top shelf of the cabinet. Boxes of cereal go on the bottom shelf. Bread goes in the breadbox. Toothpaste belongs in the bathroom. Where will you put the fruit and vegetables? They might go into the refrigerator or maybe in a bowl on the kitchen table.

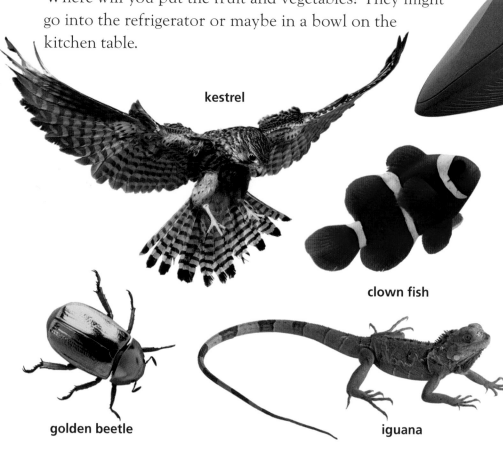

kestrel

clown fish

golden beetle

iguana

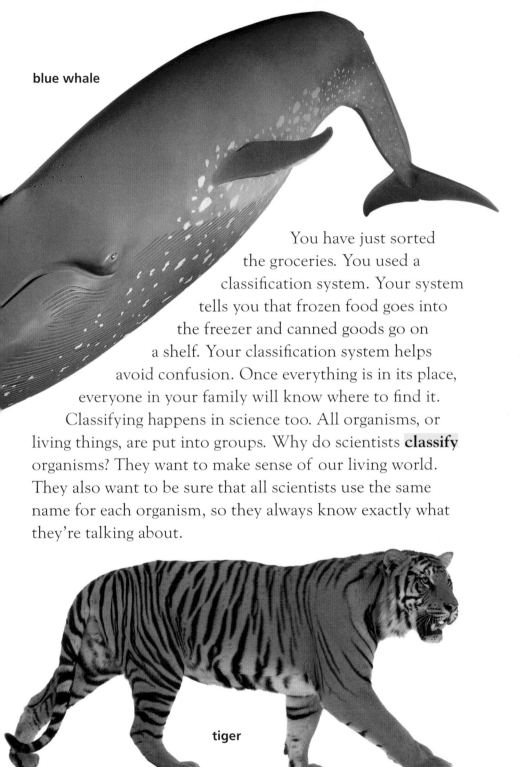

blue whale

You have just sorted the groceries. You used a classification system. Your system tells you that frozen food goes into the freezer and canned goods go on a shelf. Your classification system helps avoid confusion. Once everything is in its place, everyone in your family will know where to find it.

Classifying happens in science too. All organisms, or living things, are put into groups. Why do scientists **classify** organisms? They want to make sense of our living world. They also want to be sure that all scientists use the same name for each organism, so they always know exactly what they're talking about.

tiger

kingdom

phylum

class

Aristotle

History of The Classification System

More than two thousand years ago, a man named Aristotle came up with one of the first classifying systems. He looked at organisms and decided whether they were plants or animals. It was the first step in ordering living things.

About five hundred years ago, scientists started using Latin as the language for naming organisms. They chose Latin because it was a language that scientists from many different countries knew. Modern scientists still use it for the same reason.

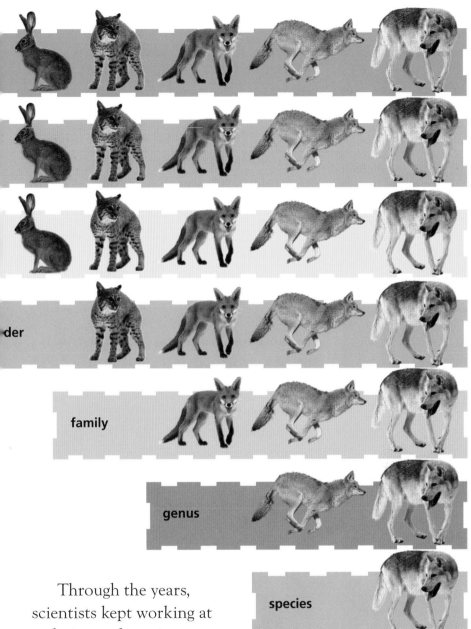

der

family

genus

species

Through the years, scientists kept working at ordering and naming organisms. The classification system used by many scientists today has seven levels. **Kingdom** is the highest level. It is the most general group of organisms. **Species** is the lowest level. It is the most specific group of organisms.

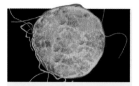

archaebacteria

eubacteria

protist

fungi

plant

Kingdom

There are six kingdoms in the living world. Remember Aristotle? He classified everything into the huge kingdoms of plants and animals. This two-kingdom system worked pretty well until the microscope was invented. Then scientists discovered tiny, single-celled organisms that were neither plants nor animals. In the nineteenth century, a German scientist came up with a third kingdom for these living things. He called them protists.

There have been more discoveries since then. Now many scientists agree that there are six kingdoms. The two we've already mentioned are the plant and animal kingdoms. There are also protists, fungi, eubacteria, and archaebacteria.

animal

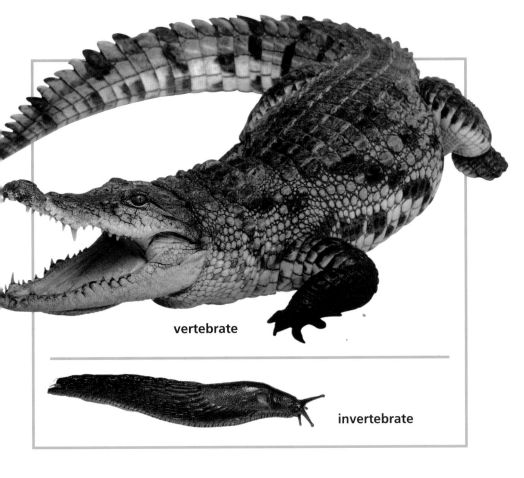

vertebrate

invertebrate

Phylum and Class

Level two is called **phylum.** In the animal kingdom
you'll find the phylum chordata with the subphylum of
vertebrates, or animals with a backbone. Then there are
the many phyla of **invertebrates,** or animals without a
backbone. The mollusk phylum contains snails and slugs.
The annelid phylum contains certain kinds of worms.

Class is the level under phylum. The five classes in
the vertebrate subphylum are mammals, reptiles, birds,
amphibians, and fish. What about all those invertebrates
such as spiders and insects and lobsters? Well, they are each
a class in the largest phylum called arthropods.

Order

There are four more levels to go in the classification system. The next one is order. These groups are based on their differences. For example, birds are a class, but the class is divided into orders of birds that perch, birds that are woodpeckers, and birds that are penguins. They are all birds, but each order is different from the others.

chaffinch

woodpecker

penguin

Family, Genus, and Species

The last three levels are family, genus, and species. In a family, all the members look alike in important ways and have similar characteristics. Members of one family might all have webbed feet or long necks. Genus is a smaller group within the family. Species is the lowest and most specific level.

Felis domestica

Felis cougar

Felis leo

Scientific Names

It is the last two levels, genus and species, that give each animal and plant its scientific name. Here's how the naming system works. *Felis*, the Latin word for cat, is the genus that includes big and small cats. *Felis* plus the species name tell us that the house cat is *Felis domestica*. The cougar is *Felis cougar*. The lion is *Felis leo*.

The Animal Kingdom

How does each organism get put into its correct group? A scientist looks at a plant or an animal very carefully and compares it with others. The scientist wants to find out how the plant or animal is like other species and how it is different. Scientists study an organism's life cycle to find out more about it. A life cycle is a pattern of birth, growth, reproduction, and death.

Is the organism made up of more than one cell? Does it get energy by eating other organisms? Does it move on its own? If yes, then it's in the animal kingdom. Does the animal have a backbone? Yes, so it's in the subphylum of vertebrates. Does the animal breathe air with lungs and make milk for its young? Does the animal have hair or fur? Are its young born looking very much like the parent animals? Then it's in the class called mammals.

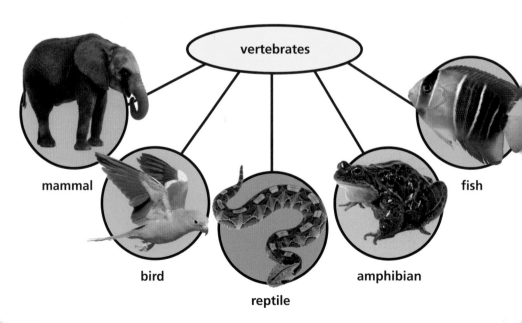

vertebrates

mammal

bird

reptile

amphibian

fish

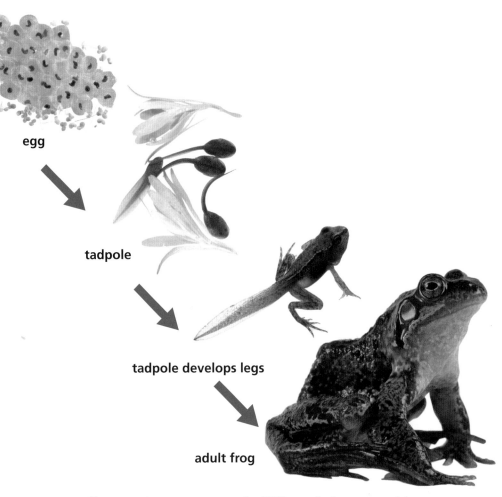

egg

tadpole

tadpole develops legs

adult frog

Not all animals are mammals. What if the animal has lungs for breathing air like a mammal, but it doesn't have fur or hair? Instead it has dry skin with scales. It is cold-blooded and its young hatch from eggs. An animal like this belongs to the reptile class.

What if the animal has feathers and its young hatch from eggs? This animal is a bird.

What if you have a cold-blooded animal that looks a lot like a reptile, but its moist, soft skin absorbs water and oxygen? Its young do not look like the parents, and they go through a big change called metamorphosis. This animal must belong to the amphibian class.

Gallimimus

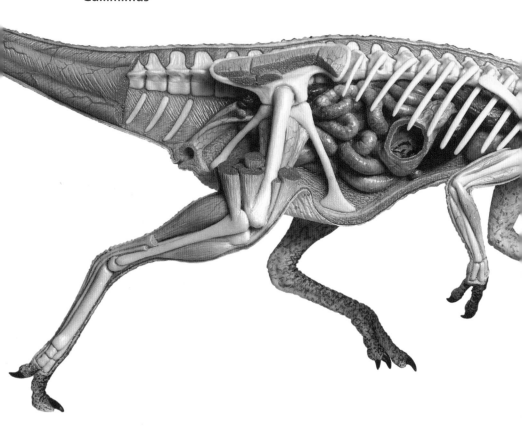

The discovery of dinosaur fossils raises many questions for scientists. These animals of long ago looked like lizards of today, which belong to the reptile class. Dinosaurs had backbones, which makes them vertebrates. They also had scales and walked on four legs. But some dinosaurs had feathers and bones like birds. Sometimes fossil finds create more questions than answers.

What if the animal you are studying has no backbone? It must be from one of the many phyla of invertebrates. In the phylum of mollusks you'll find animals with soft bodies, and often with hard shells for protection. The phylum of mollusks includes the classes of snails, slugs, clams, and octopuses.

Worms are divided into many different groups. Flatworms, roundworms, and segmented worms each have their own phylum. Worms come in all shapes and sizes. Some worms are so small they can only be seen with a microscope. Others can be longer than a car!

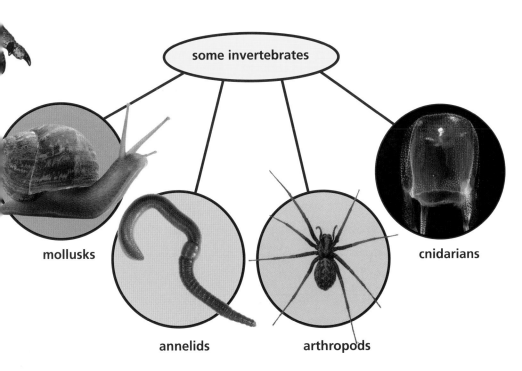

some invertebrates

mollusks

annelids

arthropods

cnidarians

The phylum Cnidaria contains jellyfish and coral. Jellyfish have very strange life cycles. They hatch from eggs and swim around for a few days or weeks. Then they attach to the ocean floor. At this stage they are called polyps. The polyp grows and bits of it fall off, forming new jellyfish.

You have probably seen a few arthropods lately. They are in the air, in our houses, and even at seafood restaurants! Arthropods are the largest phylum of animals on Earth. This phylum includes insects, spiders, and lobsters. *Arthropod* means "jointed feet." Many arthropods go through big changes during their life cycles. These changes are called metamorphosis. One example of metamorphosis is when a caterpillar turns into a butterfly.

Using a Dichotomous Key

A dichotomous key is a series of questions you can answer to figure out just what kind of organism you are looking at. There are different keys for different kinds of life forms. For example, some keys are for identifying arthropods, while others are for mammals.

The key below is for arthropods. As you answer each question on the key, you follow the correct arrow to the next question. Keep answering questions till you come to the name of the animal you are looking at. For example, the first question asks how many legs the animal has. The animal shown has eight legs, so you'll follow the arrow that says "eight." Now the key asks if the animal has claws. This animal does not have claws, so you follow the arrow to "no." This box tells you that the animal is a spider.

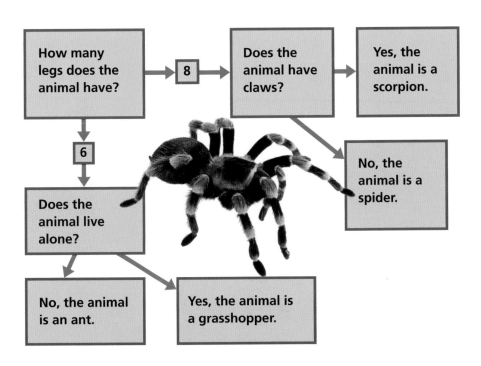

How many legs does the animal have?

8

Does the animal have claws?

Yes, the animal is a scorpion.

6

No, the animal is a spider.

Does the animal live alone?

No, the animal is an ant.

Yes, the animal is a grasshopper.

The Plant Kingdom

Does the organism you are studying use sunlight, water, and carbon dioxide to make sugar for food? If yes, then it's in the plant kingdom. Four phyla of plants that you may have seen are mosses, ferns, conifers, and flowering plants.

Mosses, which can be found on trees and along streams, have tiny leaf-like structures. They do not have flowers or seeds. Ferns grow in woodlands. They are often kept as houseplants. Ferns are vascular, which means that tubes carry food and water to the different parts of the plant. Mosses are different from ferns in that they are not vascular. Neither mosses nor ferns produce seeds. Instead, they reproduce through tiny bodies called spores.

ferns

plant

moss

fern

conifer

flowering plant

The conifer phylum includes pine trees, fir trees, and spruce trees. The needles you find on these trees are actually special leaves. Conifers are vascular like ferns, but they are different because they produce cones. The cones hold the seeds that will become new conifer trees.

Flowering plants are also vascular like ferns and conifers. As the name tells you, it is the only one of these four phyla that produces flowers. The flowers become seeds and the seeds grow into new flowering plants.

Other Kingdoms

If someone asks you to list some life forms, you'll probably start with things such as cats, dogs, monkeys, and elephants. You might also include flowers and trees. But plants and animals are really only part of the picture when talking about living things. Many scientists group life into four other kingdoms besides plants and animals. The organisms that fall into these kingdoms have some things in common with plants and animals. They all need food, water, habitats, and a way to get rid of waste. Many also need oxygen or carbon dioxide.

mushrooms

giardia lamblia

green alga

Protists

Protists are tiny life forms. Many are just a single cell. Some, like algae, live in colonies of cells. Others live inside the digestive systems of animals. Cows and termites could not survive without the protists that help them digest their food.

Fungi

You have probably seen fungi before. In fact, you've probably eaten some! These organisms include mushrooms and yeast. Many fungi look like plants, but they are not. Plants can make their own food, while fungi must absorb it from the material they grow on.

Eubacteria

Have you been sick lately? Eubacteria may be to blame! These single-celled organisms can cause illnesses like strep throat. Most eubacteria are helpful to people, though. Some of them produce vitamins. Some even help people make yogurt! Eubacteria come in many different shapes, such as spheres or spirals.

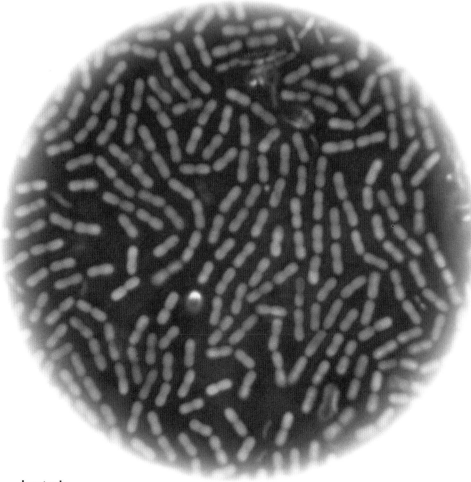

bacteria

Archaebacteria

Archaebacteria may just be the toughest things on Earth! They can survive in places that would kill any other organism. These tiny single-celled life forms do well in boiling springs where the water is full of acid. Some of them live deep in the ocean, around vents where very hot water shoots out of the Earth. This environment has no light or oxygen, and is under great pressure from the weight of the water above. The archaebacteria survive there by turning chemicals in the water into energy.

Archaebacteria living around deep sea vents provide food for other animals.

Everything is all ordered, right? Not so fast! Scientists continue to discover new organisms all the time. Sometimes they debate where the new organisms should go in the classification system. Is it a plant? Is it an animal? Is it something else? Today's scientists are still trying to put the world in order. To do this, they sometimes add to or even change the classification system. Classifying organisms helps us better understand our planet and know more about the living things in our world.

Now, let's see if you can recall the classification system of organisms. Did you remember that the different levels are kingdom, phylum, class, order, family, genus, and species? Here's a sentence that might help you: **K**ing **P**hillip **C**ome **O**ut **F**or **G**oodness' **S**ake. The first letter of each word is the same as the first letter of the level in the classification system.

Glossary

class   the level of classification below phylum

classify   to use a system to put things into groups

invertebrates   animals without backbones

kingdom   highest and most general group of organisms in the classification system

phylum   second level of classification below kingdom

species   lowest level of classification that names a particular kind of plant or animal

vertebrates   animals with backbones

What did you learn?

1. What are the benefits of a scientific classification system?

2. Which is the largest group in the classification of organisms? Which is the smallest, or most specific, group?

3. Why do scientists use Latin to name organisms?

4. **Writing** in Science The classification system originally had only two kingdoms: plant and animal. Write to explain how and why the system has changed and how it might continue to change in the future. Include details from the book to support your answer.

5. **Compare and Contrast** How are the animal kingdom and the plant kingdom alike and different?

Genre	Comprehension Skill	Text Features	Science Content
Nonfiction	Compare and Contrast	• Labels • Captions • Charts • Glossary	Classifying Organisms

Scott Foresman Science 5.1

scottforesman.com

ISBN 0-328-13917-3

9 780328 139170

90000

Physical Science

Matter and Its Properties

by Mary Miller

Vocabulary

atom

compound

concentrated

dilute

electron

element

neutron

proton

saturated

Photographs: Every effort has been made to secure permission and provide appropriate credit for photographic material. The publisher deeply regrets any omission and pledges to correct errors called to its attention in subsequent editions. Unless otherwise acknowledged, all photographs are the property of Scott Foresman, a division of Pearson Education. Photo locators denoted as follows: Top (T), Center (C), Bottom (B), Left (L), Right (R) Background (Bkgd)

Title Page: ©DK Images; 2 Courtesy of Stanford Linear Accelerator Center; 9 ©Herald Sund/Getty Images; 13 ©Spencer James/Getty Images, (C) ©Charles D. Winters; 14 (TR, CR) ©DK Images; 15(TR, CR) ©DK Images, (CR) ©Richard Megna/Fundamental Photographs; 16 ©Tom Schierlitz/Getty Images; 18 ©Paul Seheult/Eye Ubiquitous/Corbis; 19 Getty Images 23 ©DK Images

ISBN: 0-328-13946-7